BENTO BOXES
Japanese Meals on the Go

Naomi Kijima

JAPAN PUBLICATIONS TRADING CO.,LTD./GRAPH-SHA

CONTENTS

All the recipes are for 1 serving, unless otherwise specified.

Measurements used in this book:

1 cup=200ml 1 tablespoon(Tbsp)=15ml 1 teaspoon(tsp)=5ml

Sake, Mirin, and **Dashi stock** are essential to Japanese cooking.

◆Sake (rice wine) mellows food, tones down raw taste or smells and improves flavor. Dry sherry can be a substitute for sake.

◆Mirin (sweet cooking rice wine) is used to improve flavor and give food glaze and sweetness. Mirin may be substituted with 1 tablespoon sake and 1 teaspoon sugar.

◆Dashi stock is made from konbu and bonito flakes. You may also use commercial dashi stocks.

About the author:
Naomi Kijima is a well known cookbook author and teacher in Japan. She has appeared on Japanese television and her recipes are regularly featured in women's magazines and newspapers there.

TRADITIONAL JAPANESE FAVORITES

From teriyaki to sushi, these time-honored recipes are sure to please every palate.

Yellowtail Teriyaki

1 piece yellowtail
Salt and pepper to taste
Pastry flour for dredging
$\frac{1}{2}$ Tbsp cooking oil
2 tsp each sake and mirin
$\frac{1}{2}$ tsp sugar
2 tsp soy sauce

1. Slice the yellowtail into bite-sized pieces. Season with salt and pepper.
2. Dredge lightly in the flour and sauté in the cooking oil (Fig. 1).
3. Combine the sake, sugar, and mirin, add to the pan (Fig. 2), and cook over low heat until reduced by half.
4. Drizzle soy sauce in pan. Shake the pan gently until the fish is coated in the glaze.

Gobo

3" (8 cm) gobo (burdock root) • $\frac{1}{2}$ tsp cooking oil • $\frac{1}{2}$ tsp sesame oil • $\frac{1}{4}$ carrot, julienned • 2 tsp soy sauce • 1 tsp each sugar, mirin, and sake • 2 Tbsp water

1. Julienne the gobo into $1\frac{1}{2}$" (4 cm) lengths. Soak in cold water and drain.
2. Sauté the gobo in the two oils for 1 minute. Stir in the carrot.
3. Add the remaining ingredients and cook 2 minutes more.

Yam Noodle Salad

2 oz (50 g) shirataki (konnyaku noodles) •1 Tbsp sake • 1Tbsp water • Pinch salt • 1 Tbsp Cod Roe Sprinkles (p. 63)

1. Chop the shirataki. Parboil, and then drain.
2. Cook the shirataki over medium heat with the sake, water, and salt until the liquid has evaporated.
3. Add the Cod Roe Sprinkles and cook briefly

★ Sprinkle aonori (green seaweed sprinkles) on the rice. Sprinkle the Gobo with roasted sesame seeds. Garnish with steamed Chinese greens.

Salted Salmon

1 piece salted salmon
Broil on both sides until just golden.

Omelet

1 egg, beaten • 2 tsp sugar • $\frac{1}{2}$ tsp soy sauce • Cooking oil

1. Combine the egg, sugar, and soy sauce.
2. Heat the oil in a pan. Add the egg in a thin stream, lifting the edges, to make a fluffy omelet.
3. Slice into bite-sized pieces.

Hijiki

1 Tbsp hijiki (edible brown algae) • $\frac{1}{3}$ aburage (tofu puff) • $\frac{1}{4}$ carrot, julienned • 1 tsp cooking oil • 4 Tbsp dashi stock • 2 tsp soy sauce • $\frac{1}{2}$ tsp sugar

1. Soak the hijiki in water, drain, and chop. Rinse the aburage in boiling water and julienne.
2. Sauté the hijiki, aburage, and carrot in the oil. Add the remaining ingredients and simmer for 3–4 minutes.

Lotus Root Salad

2 oz (50 g) lotus root • 1 dried red pepper • $\frac{1}{2}$ Tbsp vinegar • $\frac{1}{2}$ Tbsp sugar • 2 Tbsp water • Salt

1. Peel the lotus root. Slice into thin half rounds. Soak in cold water, then drain. Remove the seeds from the red pepper and slice crosswise into rings.
2. Bring all the other ingredients to a boil. Add the pepper and lotus root and boil for 2–3 minutes over high heat.

★ Place the Salmon and Egg on top of the rice. Garnish with sliced steamed snow peas.

Crispy Mackerel

¹/₂ slice mackerel
¹/₂ Tbsp soy sauce
¹/₂ tsp juice from grated ginger
Cornstarch for dredging
2–3 sweet peppers
Oil for deep-frying

1. Score the mackerel in several places. Slice into ¹/₂"-thick (1.5 cm) pieces. Marinate for 10 minutes in the soy sauce and ginger liquid.

2. Make vertical slits in the sweet pepper and deep fry in oil at 320° F (160° C).

3. Pat the mackerel dry. Dredge in plenty of cornstarch. Tap off the excess (Fig. 1) and deep fry in oil at 340° F (170° C) oil (Fig. 2).

Stir-Fried Turnip Greens

1 handful turnip greens • 1 tsp young sardines (chirimenjako) • Cooking oil • 1 Tbsp water • Salt

1. Blanch the greens in salted water until just tender. Rinse in cold water and chop.

2. Sauté the young sardines in the cooking oil. Add the salt and water. Stir in the turnip leaves.

Soy Sauce Eggs

1 hard-boiled egg, peeled • Soy sauce

Marinate the egg in a small dish of soy sauce, turning occasionally, until the surface is light brown all over. Slice into quarters lengthwise.

★Place the Stir-Fried Turnip Greens on top of the rice. Pack the Crispy Mackerel and the Soy Sauce Eggs in the other container, and garnish with Chrysanthemum Turnips (p. 61).

Chicken Thighs Teriyaki

½ **boneless chicken thigh, skin on (5 oz / 150 g)**
1 Tbsp each mirin and soy sauce
1 tsp sugar
½ Tbsp cooking oil
2–3 spears asparagus

1. Trim excess fat from thigh. Marinate in the mirin, soy sauce, and sugar for 30 minutes. Drain, reserving marinade, and pat dry.
2. Cook the chicken in the oil, skin side down. When browned, turn and cook the other side.
3. Add 3 Tbsp *water* to the reserved marinade and pour over the chicken (Fig. 1). Cover and simmer until cooked through. Remove the cover, raise the heat, and reduce the sauce to a glaze (Fig. 2). Slice.
4. Blanch the asparagus in salted water. Chop.
5. Toss chicken and asparagus in the glaze.

Quick Cabbage Pickles

1 leaf Chinese cabbage • ½ tsp salt

Julienne the green portion of the Chinese cabbage. Slice the white portion length wise into thin strips. Sprinkle with salt, knead well, and squeeze out the liquid.

★ Place the Chicken and asparagus on the rice. Garnish with red pickled ginger and the quick pickles.

Pan-Fried Chicken

4" (10 cm) gobo (burdock root), peeled and chopped

³/₄" (2 cm) lotus root, chopped

¹/₄ konnyaku (devil's tongue jelly), diced

2–3 string beans

¹/₄ boneless skinless chicken thigh, sliced

2 tsp cooking oil

1¹/₂" (4 cm) carrot, chopped

1¹/₂ Tbsp soy sauce

2 tsp sugar

2 tsp mirin

2 tsp sake

Salt

1. Boil the gobo until tender and plunge in cold water. Soak the lotus root in cold water. Parboil the konnyaku. Blanch the string beans and chop.

2. Sauté the chicken in the oil. Add the carrots (Fig. 1). Stir in the konnyaku and gobo. Add ¹/₃ cup *water* and boil 2–3 minutes.

3. Add the remaining ingredients. Cook for 7–8 minutes. Stir in the lotus root and string beans and reduce the liquid to a sauce (Fig. 2).

Wakame Stir Fry

2 Tbsp (5 g) wakame (low salt) • 1 slice fresh ginger, julienned • 1 Tbsp cooking oil • 1 tsp sake • 1 tsp light soy sauce

1. Wash the wakame and chop.

2. Sauté the wakame and ginger in the oil. Add the sake and soy sauce.

★ Top the rice with umeboshi (pickled plum). Garnish with persimmon slices.

Miso-Marinated Pork

2 pieces pork loin (4 oz / 100 g)
2 tsp miso
1 tsp each mirin, sake, and sugar

1. Trim the pork. Combine the remaining ingredients and rub onto the pork. Marinate 20–30 minutes or overnight.
2. Scrape off and reserve the miso marinade (Fig. 1) and broil or grill the pork.
3. When the pork is fully cooked, brush the reserved marinade on the pork and continue grilling until golden (Fig. 2). Slice.

Stewed Konnyaku

¼ konnyaku (devil's tongue jelly) • 1 Tbsp soy sauce • 1 tsp each mirin, sugar, and sake • 4 Tbsp water • Bonito flakes

1. Cut the konnyaku into ¼"-thick (5 mm) slices, then cut each slice in half lengthwise. Make a slit in each slice and pull one end through the slit for a twist shape. Parboil and drain.
2. Cook in the mirin, sugar, sake, and water until the liquid is absorbed (4–5 minutes). Stir in the bonito flakes.

Sautéed Green Pepper

½ green pepper • Cooking oil • Salt
Julienne the pepper and sauté in the oil.

Season with salt.

Soy Carrot

2" (5 cm) carrot • 1 Tbsp soy sauce
Slice the carrot in half lengthwise. Score the slices deeply, making the cuts close together. Drizzle with soy sauce and let stand 30 minutes. Chop.

★ Sprinkle the rice with black sesame seeds and tuck the other items alongside.

Ginger Pork

4 oz (100 g) thinly sliced pork
1 Tbsp soy sauce
1 tsp grated fresh ginger
1/2 Tbsp cooking oil

1. Cut pork slices into bite-sized pieces. Marinate in soy sauce and ginger (Fig. 1).

2. Cook pork slices in the oil, over high heat, on both sides (Fig. 2).

Simmered Pumpkin

3 oz (80 g) pumpkin • 1 Tbsp sugar • 1 tsp light soy sauce

1. Dice pumpkin in 3/4" (2 cm) cubes. Shave off the sharp edges.

2. Boil in a small amount of *water* for 4–5 minutes.

3. Add the sugar and continue cooking. When tender, drizzle with soy sauce.

Sesame Spinach

4 oz (100 g) spinach • 1 Tbsp crushed black sesame seeds • 1/2 Tbsp soy sauce • 1 tsp sugar

1. Blanch the spinach briefly in salted water. Drain and chop.

2. Combine the remaining ingredients and toss with the spinach.

Quick Mushrooms

1/2 Tbsp soy sauce • 1 tsp mirin • 3 Tbsp water • 3/4 oz (20 g) shimeji mushrooms, in stalks

Bring liquid ingredients to a boil and add the shimeji. Cook briefly, then drain.

★Sprinkle the shimeji on the rice. Place the pork on lettuce leaves.

Beef Sukiyaki

3 oz (80 g) paper-thin beef
2 oz (50 g) shirataki (konnyaku noodles), chopped
8–9 yaki-fu (roasted wheat-gluten bread)
$1/2$ Tbsp cooking oil
$1 1/2$ Tbsp soy sauce
2 tsp each sugar, mirin, and sake
4" (10 cm) naganegi (Japanese bunching onion), sliced diagonally
$1/4$ carrot, julienned

1. Cut beef into 1" (3 cm) strips. Parboil the shirataki. Soak the yaki-fu in cold water and drain.
2. Sauté the shirataki in the cooking oil, and then add the beef (Fig. 1).
3. Add $2/3$ cup *water* and bring to a boil. Stir in the soy sauce, sugar, mirin, and sake. Add the naganegi, carrot, and yaki-fu and cook 4–5 minutes (Fig. 2).

Sautéed Greens

5 leaves daikon greens • 2 tsp dried shrimp (sakura-ebi) • 1 tsp cooking oil • Salt

1. Boil daikon greens in salted water till almost tender. Rinse in cold water, drain, and chop.
2. Sauté the shrimp in the oil. Stir in the greens. Salt to taste.

Daikon Salad

1" (3 cm) daikon • Salt • 1 Tbsp vinegar • 1 tsp sugar • Citron juice • $1/4$ tsp citron zest, julienned

1. Peel the daikon and slice into quarter rounds. Sprinkle with salt, knead well, and squeeze out the liquid.
2. Combine the vinegar, sugar, and citron juice. Marinate the daikon slices and citron zest in the sweetened vinegar for 10 minutes.

For paper-thin beef, ask for sukiyaki meat at a Japanese specialty store. To serve, top the rice with the sukiyaki. The other items can be placed in paper or aluminum cupcake wrappers.

Glazed Meatball.

1/4 onion, minced
1/2 tsp cooking oil
3 oz (80 g) ground beef
2 tsp beaten egg
2 Tbsp breadcrumbs
Salt and pepper
Oil for deep-frying
2 tsp soy sauce
1/2 tsp each sugar, mirin, and sake
3 Tbsp water
4 quail's eggs, hard-boiled

1. Sauté the onion in the oil until translucent. Let cool.
2. Combine the ground beef, cooked onion, beaten egg, breadcrumbs, salt, and pepper.
3. Knead well (Fig. 1). Form into small balls.
4. Deep fry at 340° F (170° C) for 2–3 minutes until well browned (Fig. 2).
5. Place meatballs in a pan with all remaining ingredients except the quail eggs. Boil 4–5 minutes.
6. Place the meatballs on short skewers, alternating with quail eggs.

★Sprinkle the rice with Cod Roe Sprinkles (p. 63). Garnish the meatball skewers with quick-steamed broccoli spears and sliced apple.

Beef Rolls

4 oz (100 g) thinly sliced beef
4" (10 cm) gobo (burdock root)
4" (10 cm) carrot, sliced in quarters
   lengthwise
$1/3$ cup dashi stock
$1\frac{1}{2}$ Tbsp soy sauce
1 Tbsp mirin
4 string beans, blanched
Pastry flour
1 tsp cooking oil
1 tsp each sugar and sake
3 Tbsp water
Salt

1. Scrape the gobo. Julienne into 6–8 pieces and blanch. Julienne the carrot into $1/4$"-thick (5 mm) pieces. Combine with the gobo and boil with the dashi, $1/2$ *Tbsp* of the soy sauce, and $1/2$ *Tbsp* of the mirin for 3–4 minutes.

2. Stack 2–3 slices of meat. Sprinkle with the flour and stack with half of the vegetables (Figure). Roll tightly. Repeat with remaining meat and vegetables.

3. Heat the oil in a skillet. Place the meat rolls in the skillet, seam down. Brown on all sides. Add the sugar, sake, water, and the remaining soy sauce and mirin. Cook until glazed. Cut rolls crosswise into bite-sized cylinders.

Sweet Potatoes

3 oz (80 g) sweet potato, peeled • 1 Tbsp sugar • 1 tsp soy sauce

1. Cut the sweet potato into $3/4$"-thick (2 cm) rounds. Rinse in cold water.

2. Boil until just tender in $1/3$ cup *water*. Add sugar and cook 2–3 more minutes. Drizzle with soy sauce.

Spicy Shimeji and Lettuce

1 oz (30 g) shimeji mushroom • 2–3 leaves green leaf lettuce • $1/2$ tsp cooking oil • 1 tsp soy sauce • 1 tsp sake • Pinch shichimi-togarashi (7-spice powder)

1. Trim the roots of the shimeji and separate into stalks. Cut lettuce into large pieces.

2. Sauté the shimeji in the oil. Add the soy sauce and sake. When hot, toss the lettuce quickly in the pan and remove from heat. Sprinkle with the shichimi-togarashi.

★ For thinly sliced beef, ask for sukiyaki meat at a Japanese specialty store. To serve, garnish with Stewed Konbu (p. 61) sprinkled with roasted sesame seeds.

Chicken Dumplings

3 oz (80 g) ground chicken
2 tsp pastry flour
2 tsp cornstarch
1 tsp beaten egg
Minced naganegi (Japanese bunching onion)
Salt and pepper
2 green shiso leaves
1 piece roasted seaweed, cut into 3" squares (8 cm)
1/2 tsp cooking oil

1. Combine the chicken, flour, cornstarch, egg, naganegi, salt, and pepper. Knead well.

2. Divide the chicken mixture into four half circles. Wrap two with the shiso leaves (Fig. 1) and two with the seaweed.

3. Cook the dumplings in the oil, turning, until golden brown on both sides (Fig. 2). Lower the heat to medium and continue cooking 2 more minutes until cooked through.

Teriyaki Scallops

5 scallops • 1 Tbsp soy sauce • 1 tsp sugar • 1 tsp sake • 1 Tbsp water

1. Trim the scallops.

2. Bring the remaining ingredients to a boil. Add the scallops and cook 3–4 minutes until well glazed.

Sautéed Asparagus

3 spears asparagus • Cooking oil • Salt and pepper

1. Trim the asparagus and blanch in salted water. Cut into 2" (5 cm) lengths.

2. Sauté briefly in oil. Add salt and pepper.

★ Serve with Adzuki Beans (p. 59).

Oyako Don

4 oz (100 g) chicken thigh meat
$\frac{1}{4}$ onion, sliced thin
$1\frac{1}{3}$ Tbsp soy sauce
$1\frac{1}{3}$ Tbsp mirin
1 tsp sugar
$\frac{1}{3}$ cup water
$\frac{1}{3}$ bunch mitsuba (honewort)
1 beaten egg

1. Cut the chicken into bite-sized pieces.
2. Add all other ingredients except the mitsuba and egg. Boil for 3–4 minutes (Fig. 1).

3. Chop the mitsuba and stir in. Add the egg in a thin stream, turning pan (Fig. 2). Cook until eggs are nearly set.

Gobo in Vinegar

$4\frac{3}{4}$" (12 cm) gobo (burdock root), peeled • $\frac{1}{3}$ cup dashi stock • $1\frac{1}{2}$ Tbsp vinegar • 2 tsp sugar • Salt • Roasted sesame seeds

1. Cut the gobo crosswise into 3 pieces. Slice lengthwise and blanch.
2. Stir in the dashi, vinegar, sugar, and salt. Cook for 5 minutes. Sprinkle with the sesame seeds.

Komatsuna Stir Fry

1 Tbsp young sardines (chirimenjako) • 4 oz (100 g) komatsuna (a kind of Chinese cabbage), chopped • $\frac{1}{2}$ Tbsp cooking oil • Salt

1. Dry-roast the young sardines in a skillet.
2. Add the oil. Stir in the komatsuna. Salt to taste.

★To serve, sprinkle the rice with chopped pieces of roasted seaweed. Spoon the Oyako on top. Add the vegetable items.

Chikuwa Teriyaki

1/2 **stick yaki-chikuwa**
 (broiled fish-cake tube)
2 small pieces satsuma-age (deep-
 fried fish-paste cake)
1/2 **Tbsp cooking oil**
1 1/2 **Tbsp soy sauce**
1/2 **Tbsp each sugar, mirin, and sake**
1/3 **cup water**
Pinch roasted black sesame seeds

1. Slice the chikuwa into 1/3"-thick (7–8
mm) diagonal rings. Cut the satsuma-
age into bite-sized pieces.

2. Sauté the chikuwa and satsuma-age in
the oil (Fig. 1). Add all the other ingredients except the sesame seeds. Stirring
occasionally, cook for 3–4 minutes or
until well glazed (Fig. 2).

Sprinkle with sesame seeds.

Sautéed Shrimp and Okra

2 shrimp, peeled and deveined • 2 okra •
1 oz (30 g) enoki mushrooms • 1 tsp
cooking oil • 1 tsp sake • Salt

1. Parboil the shrimp and chop into 3–4
pieces each. Slice the okra in half on
the diagonal. Divide the enoki mushrooms into small clumps.

2. Sauté the enoki and okra in the oil.
Add the shrimp and cook briefly. Stir in
the sake and salt.

Seaweed-Wrapped Hanpen

1/2 **hanpen • Soy sauce to taste • 1/2 roast-**
ed seaweed

1. Slice the hanpen into 1/2"- thick (1.5
cm) sticks. Place on a rack over a burner.
Brush with soy sauce and grill until gold-
en brown.

2. Cut the seaweed into 1/3"-wide (1 cm)
strips. Wrap around the middles of the
hanpen.

★ Spoon the Chikuwa Teriyaki on top of
the rice. Add the other two side items
and garnish with sliced strawberries.

Inari-zushi and Maki-zushi

1 cup (180 cc) uncooked rice
2 Tbsp vinegar
3 Tbsp sugar
2 aburage (tofu puffs)
1 yard (1 m) dried gourd (kampyo)
1²/₃ Tbsp soy sauce
1 tsp each mirin and sake
¹/₂ cup water
1 egg, beaten
Salt • Cooking oil
2 oz (50 g) spinach
¹/₂ piece roasted seaweed

1. Cook the rice according to manufacturer's directions. Combine the vinegar with *2 tsp* of the sugar and *¹/₃ tsp* of the salt. Pour over the rice and stir with a cutting motion.

2. Rinse the aburage with boiling water and then cut in half crosswise. Carefully open and make a pouch. Soften the kampyo by rubbing with salt. Cut into 6" (15 cm) lengths and parboil, then drain. Place in a pot with the soy sauce, *1¹/₂ Tbsp* of the sugar, the mirin, the sake, and the water. Cook over low heat for 10 minutes.

3. Add the remaining sugar and a pinch of salt to the beaten egg. Heat the oil in a square pan. Make a long, thin omelet.

4. Blanch the spinach in salted water. Gently squeeze out the water.

5. Divide half of the rice into three portions. Stuff the rice tightly into each pouch of the aburage and fold the edges over the pouch and shape. (Inari-zushi).

6. Place the roasted seaweed on a sushi rolling mat, short side toward you. Spread the remaining rice on top, leaving about 1" of seaweed at the end farthest from you. Place the kampyo, egg, and spinach on the rice (Figure) and roll until you reach the end of the rice. Wet the remaining seaweed with a few drops of water and finish rolling (Maki-zushi).

Broccoli Sauté

1¹/₂ oz (40 g) broccoli florets • 1 slice ham • ¹/₂ tsp soy sauce • Cooking oil • Salt
Blanch the broccoli in boiling salted water. Cut the ham into bite-sized pieces. Sauté with the broccoli in the oil. Add the soy sauce.

Sweet Marinated Myoga

2 myoga (Japanese ginger) • 2 Tbsp vinegar • 1 tsp sugar • Salt
Cut the myoga in half lengthwise. Boil until just tender. Marinate in the other ingredients.

★The Inari-zushi and Maki-zushi go in the container first. Using a lettuce leaf underneath, tuck the Broccoli Sauté in one corner. Place the myoga in another corner with freshly sliced cucumber.

Chicken-Tofu Rice *(For multiple servings)*

2 cups (360 cc) uncooked rice
4 oz (100 g) boneless skinless
  chicken breast
1 aburage (tofu puffs)
2 Tbsp hijiki (edible brown algae)
$1^1/_2$" (4 cm) carrots
$2^1/_2$ Tbsp soy sauce
1 Tbsp sake
$^1/_2$ Tbsp mirin

1. Wash and drain the rice.
2. Cut the chicken into $^1/_3$" (1 cm) dice. Rinse the aburage with boiling water and julienne. Rinse the hijiki and soak in water. Cut into short lengths. Cut the carrots in half crosswise, then into matchsticks.
3. Place the rice in a rice cooker. Add the soy sauce, sake, and mirin (Fig. 1). Add the amount of water specified by the man-ufacturer. Add the ingredients from Step 2 (Fig. 2) and start the rice cooker.
4. When finished, allow the rice to steam for a few more minutes. Open and stir gently.

Sautéed Chicken and Snow Peas

1 oz (30 g) snow peas • 2 oz (50 g) chicken breast • Salt and pepper • Cooking oil

1. Remove the stems of the snow peas and blanch in boiling salted water. Dice the chicken into $^1/_3$" (1 cm) pieces.
2. Sauté the chicken in the oil until golden in brown. Stir in the snow peas. Season with salt and pepper.

★ Pack the Chicken-Tofu Rice in the contain-er. Spoon the sautéed chicken and snow peas next to the rice. Garnish with half of an orange.

Rice Balls
4 Varieties of Rice Balls

1 pound (500 g) cooked rice
Beef **Ginger to taste, julienned**
    1 Tbsp soy sauce
    1 tsp each sugar, mirin, sake
    1 Tbsp water
    2 oz (50 g) beef, sliced thin
Egg **1 small egg, beaten**
    2 tsp sugar
    Salt • Cooking oil
Konbu **Stewed Konbu (p. 61)**
    Roasted sesame seeds
Umeboshi **1 umeboshi**

1. Combine all the ingredients of the beef section except the beef. Bring to a boil in a small pan. Cut the beef into narrow strips and add to the pan. Cook for 3–4 minutes and set aside.

2. Combine all the egg ingredients except the oil. Heat the oil in a pan. Add the egg mixture. Scramble, stirring rapidly, until the egg has separated into small, round pieces.

3. Julienne the Stewed Konbu.

4. Remove the seed of the umeboshi and shred the umeboshi into small pieces.

5. Divide the rice in four portions. Combine each portion with a different mixture (beef; egg; konbu, Fig.1; umeboshi). Form into flattened balls (Fig. 2).

String Beans

2 oz (50 g) string beans • ⅓ cup dashi stock • 2 tsp soy sauce • ⅔ tsp each mirin, sake, and sugar

String the beans. Cut into 1" (3 cm) lengths. Boil in all the other ingredients for 5–6 minutes, stirring occasionally.

★ For paper-thin beef, ask for sukiyaki meat at a Japanese specialty market. To serve, place the Onigiri in the container with the String Beans and garnish with grapes.

Crisp-Frying

Rice Cracker Tempura

2 shrimp • Small amount of pastry flour and beaten egg • Miniature rice crackers (see p. 40) • Oil for deep frying

1. Peel the shrimp except for the last segment and the tail. Devein. Make an incision on the underside.

2. Combine the flour, egg, and crackers to make a batter and coat the shrimp. Fry at 340° F (170° C) until crisp.

Scallop Clusters

Small amount of lotus root • 10 mitsuba leaves • 2 Tbsp pastry flour • 1 quail's egg, beaten • 1 Tbsp water • 1 oz (30 g) scallops • Oil for deep frying

1. Chop the lotus root and mitsuba leaves. Combine the flour, egg, and water to form the batter.

2. Stir the scallops, lotus root, and mitsuba in the batter. Drop the scallop mixture by thirds into 340° F (170° C) oil, making three clusters. Fry until crisp, turning frequently.

Rice Cracker Tempura

Scallop Clusters

Chikuwa Clusters

Seasoned Chicken

Seasoned Chicken

4 oz (100 g) boneless skinless chicken thigh • Minced ginger and naganegi (Japanese bunching onion) • ½ Tbsp sake • ½ Tbsp soy sauce • 1 heaping Tbsp cornstarch • Oil for deep-frying

1. Cut the chicken into bite-sized pieces. Combine all the ingredients except cornstarch and oil. Marinate the chicken in the ginger mixture for 5 minutes.

2. Dredge the chicken in the cornstarch. Fry at 350° F (175° C) until golden and crisp.

Chikuwa Clusters

1½" (4 cm) yaki-chikuwa (broiled fish-cake tubes) • 1 Tbsp pastry flour • 1 quail's egg • Pinch aonori (green seaweed sprinkles)

1. Cut the chikuwa in half diagonally.

2. Combine the flour and egg. Coat each piece of chikuwa in the batter and sprinkle with the aonori. Fry at 350° F (175° C) until golden.

For an easy way to expand your bento repertoire, try replacing the main item with one of these colorful creations.

Grilling

Salt-Roasted Cuttlefish

1/4 cuttlefish • Splash of sake • Salt

1. Marinate the squid briefly in the sake and salt. Pat dry.

2. Grill or broil on a rack until golden. Cut into bite-sized pieces.

Miso Cod

2 Tbsp sake dregs (sake-kasu) • 1 1/2 Tbsp miso • 1/2 tsp sugar • 1 cod fillet • Salt

1. Leave the sake dregs at room temperature to soften. Combine with the miso and sugar. Sprinkle salt on the cod and spread the miso mixture all over. Wrap in plastic wrap and chill overnight.

2. Scrape off the excess miso mixture and grill on a rack until golden brown.

Miso Cod

Salt-Roasted Cuttlefish

Two-Color Chicken Wings

Miso Beef

Miso Beef

1 1/2 Tbsp miso • 1 tsp each mirin, sugar and sake • 4 oz (100 g) round steak

1. Combine the miso, mirin, sugar, and sake and spread on the beef. Wrap in plastic wrap and chill overnight.

2. Scrape the miso mixture off the beef. Grill or broil until medium rare. Slice into strips.

Two-Color Chicken Wings

2 chicken wings • Salt • Aonori (green seaweed sprinkles) • Shichimi-togarashi (7-spice powder)

1. Cut the wings in two at the joint. Sprinkle with salt.

2. Grill or broil until fully cooked, at least 4–5 minutes. Sprinkle one piece with aonori; the other with shichimi-togarashi.

Pan-Frying

Beef and Mushroom Stir Fry

4 oz (100 g) beef, sliced paper thin • Salt and pepper • 1½ tsp cooking oil • 2 oz (50 g) enoki mushrooms • 1 oz (30 g) shimeji mushrooms, in stalks • 1 tsp soy sauce • 1 tsp sake

1. Cut the beef in thin strips and toss with the salt, the pepper, and *½ tsp* of the oil. Set aside. Trim off the root bottom of the enoki and chop.

2. Heat the remaining oil in a pan and cook the beef until nearly done. Stir in the mushrooms. Add the soy sauce and sake.

Tricolor Vegetable Julienne

½ potato • 1 green pepper • ⅓ carrot • ½ Tbsp cooking oil • Salt and pepper

1. Julienne all the vegetables with a mandoline. Soak the potato pieces in cold water, then drain well.

2. Heat the oil in a frying pan. Stir in the carrot first, then the potato, then the green pepper. Sprinkle with salt and pepper.

Braising

Buddha's Delight

1 taro root • Salt for rubbing • 1" (3 cm) carrot, peeled • ¼ slice of fried tofu (atsuage) • 2 sweet peppers • 1 dried shiitake mushroom, soaked in cold water for an hour • ½ cup dashi stock • 1⅓ Tbsp soy sauce • ½ Tbsp mirin • ½ Tbsp sake • 2 tsp sugar

1. Peel the taro and cut diagonally into 2 or 3 pieces. Rub with salt to remove the stickiness. Cut the carrot into 4 pieces lengthwise and trim off the sharp corners. Rinse the atsuage with boiling water. Cut the sweet pepper in half diagonally and blanch. Cut the shiitake at an angle.

2. Bring all the other ingredients to a boil. Lower the heat and add all the ingredients from step 1 except the sweet pepper. Cook for 10 minutes, then add the sweet pepper.

Miso-Braised Chicken

1 oz (30 g) boiled bamboo shoot • 1 dried shiitake mushroom, soaked in cold water for an hour • 3 oz (80 g) chicken thigh meat • ¾" (2 cm) carrot • 4" (10 cm) naganegi (Japanese bunching onion) • ½ Tbsp cooking oil • 1 Tbsp miso • 1 tsp each sugar, sake, and mirin • 5 Tbsp water

1. Blanch the bamboo shoot. Dice the bamboo shoot, shiitake, carrot and chicken into ½" (1.5 cm) pieces. Cut the naganegi into ½" (1.5 cm) lengths and blanch.

2. Sauté the chicken in the oil. Add the shiitake, bamboo shoot, and carrot, in that order. Combine all other ingredients and add to the pan. Cook for about 10 minutes, stirring occasionally. Add the naganegi and cook 1 minute more.

Spicy Mackerel Sauté

½ slice mackerel • Asian hot mustard • Pastry flour • 1 Tbsp cooking oil • 4 oz (100 g) broccoli • Salt • 1 tsp soy sauce • 1 tsp sake

1. Slice the mackerel ½" (1.5 cm) thick. Make a slit in the skin of each piece and insert the hot mustard. Dredge lightly in the flour and sauté in *½ Tbsp* of the oil. Remove from pan.

2. Cut the broccoli into bite-sized pieces. Boil in salted water until almost tender.

3. Cook the broccoli in the remaining oil. Add the mackerel, soy sauce, and sake.

Miso Fish Cake Sauté

1 piece satsuma-age (deep-fried fish-paste cake) • 2 oz (50 g) thinly sliced pork • 2 cabbage leaves • 1 green pepper • 1 dried red chili pepper, minced • ½ Tbsp oil • 1 Tbsp miso • 1 tsp each soy sauce, mirin, sake, and sugar • 1 Tbsp water

1. Cut the satsuma-age and pork into bite-sized pieces. Slice the cabbage and green pepper into uniform squares.

2. Sauté the red pepper in the oil. Stir in the pork, then the satsuma-age, then the cabbage and green pepper. Add all the remaining ingredients and cook until the flavors are blended.

Braised Fish

4–5 small horse mackerel, smelt, or sardines (each about ½ oz; 15 g) • 1 Tbsp sake • 1 Tbsp soy sauce • ½ Tbsp vinegar • 1 tsp sugar • ½ cup water

1. Clean the fish and pat dry.

2. Bring all the other ingredients to a boil and add the fish. Cook over high heat for 4–5 minutes.

Pork and Potatoes

2 oz (50 g) pork loin, thinly sliced • 1 small potato • ¼ onion • 2 oz (50 g) shirataki (konnyaku noodles) • 2 tsp cooking oil • 1⅔ Tbsp soy sauce • ½ Tbsp sugar • 1 tsp mirin • 1 tsp sake • 1–2 snow peas • Salt

1. Slice the pork into ¾" (2 cm) strips. Cut the potato into bite-sized chunks and soak in cold water. Thinly slice the onions. Cut the shirataki into shorter lengths and parboil. Blanch the snow peas and chop. Drain the potatoes.

2. Sauté the shirataki in the oil. Add the pork, then the onion, and then the potato. Add ⅓ cup *water* and bring to a boil. Add the remaining ingredients and cook for 10 minutes. Remove from heat. Scatter with the snow peas.

EASY RICE OR NOODLE COMBINATIONS

Donburi-style cooking (rice with toppings) is well suited to bento: the flavors blend with the rice for a delicious treat even without reheating.

Cod and Vegetables

1 piece salted cod (4 oz; 100 g)
1 tsp sake
1" (3 cm) carrot
1 green pepper
1 fresh shiitake mushroom
1 Tbsp vinegar
1 Tbsp soy sauce
1/2 Tbsp sugar
3 Tbsp water
1 tsp cooking oil
Cornstarch
Oil for deep frying

1. Cut the cod at an angle and marinate in the sake. Julienne the carrot and green pepper. Remove the stem of the shiitake and slice thin.

2. Heat the oil in a pan. Stir in the carrot, green pepper, and shiitake. Add the vinegar, soy sauce, sugar, and water (Fig. 1). Bring to a boil. Dissolve *1/2 tsp* cornstarch in a little water and add to the pan to thicken.

3. Pat the cod dry and dredge in cornstarch. Deep fry at 340° F (170° C) until crisp (Fig. 2).

Sesame Greens

4 oz (100 g) shungiku (chrysanthemum leaves) • Salt • 1 Tbsp roasted sesame seeds, ground to a powder • 1/2 Tbsp soy sauce • 1 tsp sugar

1. Boil the shungiku in salted water until just tender. Drain well and chop.

2. Combine the remaining ingredients. Toss with the shungiku.

★Place the cod on the rice and pour the vegetable sauce over. Garnish with persimmon slices and the shungiku.

Miso Chicken Donburi

1/4 onion
3/4" (2 cm) carrot
1/2 green pepper
1 1/2 oz (40g) ground chicken
1 1/2 Tbsp miso
1 Tbsp sake
1/2 tsp cornstarch
1/2 Tbsp cooking oil

1. Mince the onion, carrot, and green pepper.

2. Cook the chicken in hot oil until well done. Stir in the onion and carrot (Fig. 1).

3. Add the green pepper. Stir in the miso, sake, and 2 Tbsp *water*. Cook, stirring, for 2–3 minutes.

4. Dissolve the cornstarch in a little water. Add to the pan (Fig. 2) and cook until thickened.

Spinach and Egg Sauté

3 oz (80 g) spinach • 1 egg, beaten • Salt • Pepper • 1 Tbsp cooking oil • 1/2 Tbsp soy sauce • 1/2 Tbsp sake

1. Blanch the spinach in boiling salted water. Squeeze out the water and chop. Stir the salt and pepper into the beaten egg.

2. With *1/2 Tbsp* oil in a pan, make a small omelet with the egg. Remove.

3. Add the remaining oil to the pan. Stir in the spinach. Add the soy sauce and sake.

Crunchy Cabbage and Carrots

2 leaves Chinese cabbage • Small piece of carrot, julienned • 2/3 tsp salt

1. Julienne the green cabbage leaves and their white stalks separately.

2. Sprinkle the stem strips and the carrots with the salt. Knead gently. Add the green strips and squeeze out all excess liquid.

★Top the rice with the Miso Chicken. Add the Spinach and Egg Sauté. Garnish with the Crunchy Cabbage and Carrots and sliced kiwi.

Chicken and Celery Stir Fry

2 chicken breast tenderloins
1½ tsp cooking oil
1½ tsp sake
Salt
4 pieces tree-ear fungus (kikurage),
    soaked in cold water for an hour
1 stalk celery
½ Tbsp soy sauce

1. Trim the tenderloins and slice thin. Marinate in *½ tsp* of the oil, *½ tsp* of the sake, and salt. Julienne the tree-ear fungus and the celery.

2. Sauté the chicken in the remaining oil and remove from pan (Fig. 1).

3. Sauté the celery and fungus until tender. Return the chicken to the pan. Stir in the soy sauce and sake (Fig. 2).

Roasted Cod Roe

½ sac salted cod roe

Broil until lightly browned on all sides. Cut into diagonal rounds.

Miso Cucumber

1 Japanese cucumber • 2 tsp miso • 1 tsp sake

1. Peel vertical stripes into the cucumber. Combine the miso and sake and rub on the cucumber. Let stand 30 minutes.

2. Scrape off the miso and chop.

★ To serve, top the rice with the Chicken and Celery Stir Fry. Add the other two side items.

Seafood Donburi

1 large scallop

1 1/2 **Tbsp soy sauce**

2 **tsp mirin**

3 **tsp sake**

3 **Tbsp water**

2 **prawns, deveined with a skewer
and not peeled**

2 **Tbsp fresh salmon roe**

1. Slice the scallops into three rounds. Score the rounds on the diagonal. Grill or broil over high heat, then brush with *1 tsp* of the soy sauce and grill or broil until cooked through (Fig. 1).

2. Heat *1/2 Tbsp* of the soy sauce, the mirin, *1 tsp* of the sake, and the water in a pot. Cook the prawns in the liquid for 2–3 minutes (Fig. 2). When cool,

remove the heads and the shells, leaving the tail segment on.

3. Marinate the roe in the soy sauce and sake for 2–3 hours.

Salted Cucumber

1/2 **Japanese cucumber, sliced into thin rounds • Salt • Roasted sesame seeds**

Sprinkle the salt on the cucumber rounds, knead gently, and squeeze out the liquid. Sprinkle with the sesame seeds.

★Arrange the scallops, prawns, and roe on the rice. Add Sweet Simmered Shiitake (p. 59). Garnish with the Salted Cucumber and some Lotus Root Salad (p. 4).

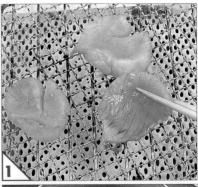

Pork and Eggplant Donburi

2¹/₂ oz (70g) thinly sliced pork
1 Japanese eggplant
1 green pepper
1¹/₂ Tbsp miso
¹/₂ Tbsp each sugar, sake, and mirin
2 Tbsp water
1 tsp cooking oil plus more for
    deep-frying

1. Cut the pork into ¹/₂"-wide (1.5 cm) strips. Peel vertical stripes into the eggplant and cut into ¹/₄"-thick (7mm) rounds. Remove the seeds from the green pepper and slice into rounds also.

2. Combine all remaining ingredients except the oil.

3. Deep fry the green pepper in 340° F

(170° C) oil and remove from the pan. Deep fry the eggplant.

4. Sauté the pork in the cooking oil. Add the miso mixture and cook for 1–2 minutes (Fig. 1).

5. With a paper towel, lightly pat the eggplant and green pepper to absorb excess oil. Combine with the pork mixture(Fig.2).

Crisped Vegetables

1¹/₂ oz (40 g) pumpkin • 1 oz (30 g) string beans, chopped • Salt • Oil for deep frying

1. Slice the pumpkin into thin wedges.

2. Deep fry the pumpkin and string beans in 340° F (170° C) oil. Sprinkle with salt.

★ Spoon the Pork and Eggplant Miso on top of the rice. Add the Crisped Vegetables and Quick Daikon-Carrot Pickles (p. 61).

DONBURI THREE WAYS

Here are three delicious varieties of donburi with egg.
Create your own new combinations.

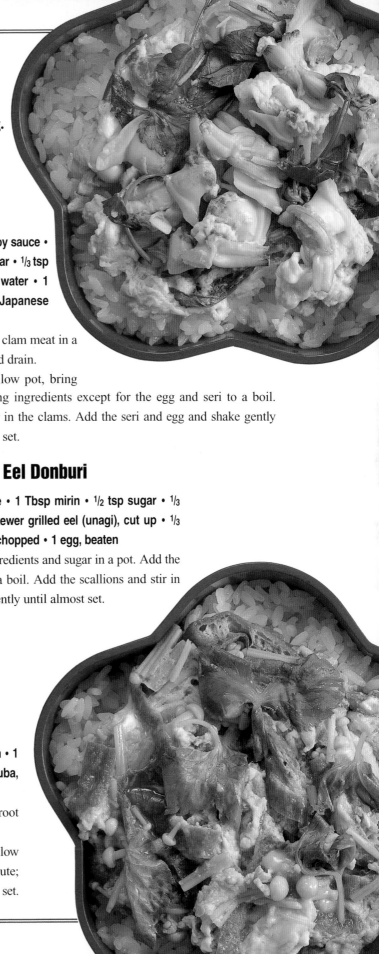

Clam Donburi

3 oz (80 g) clam meat • 2 tsp light soy sauce •
1 tsp sake • 1 tsp mirin • $^1/_2$ tsp sugar • $^1/_3$ tsp
juice from grated ginger • $^1/_3$ cup water • 1
egg, beaten • $^1/_3$ bunch seri (Japanese
parsley), chopped

1. Rinse the clam meat in a
colander and drain.
2. In a shallow pot, bring
all remaining ingredients except for the egg and seri to a boil.
Quickly stir in the clams. Add the seri and egg and shake gently
until almost set.

Eel Donburi

1 Tbsp soy sauce • 1 Tbsp mirin • $^1/_2$ tsp sugar • $^1/_3$
cup water • $^1/_2$ skewer grilled eel (unagi), cut up • $^1/_3$
bunch scallions, chopped • 1 egg, beaten

Put the liquid ingredients and sugar in a pot. Add the
eel and bring to a boil. Add the scallions and stir in
the egg. Shake gently until almost set.

Tofu Puff Donburi

1 aburage (tofu puff) • 1 oz (30 g) enoki mushrooms • 1 egg, beaten • 1
Tbsp each soy sauce, mirin, sake • 1 tsp sugar • $^1/_3$ bunch mitsuba,
chopped • $^1/_3$ cup dashi stock

1. Rinse the aburage with boiling water. Julienne. Remove the root
base of the enoki and chop.
2. Put the liquid ingredients, sugar, and tofu puff rounds in a shallow
pan and cook for 2–3 minutes. Add the enoki and cook 1 minute;
then add the mitsuba. Stir in the egg and shake gently until almost set.

Horse Mackerel Mixed Sushi

1 piece dried horse mackerel (aji)
2 green shiso leaves
1¹/₂ Tbsp vinegar
2 tsp sugar
Salt
9 oz (250 g) hot cooked rice
Roasted black sesame seeds

1. Grill the horse mackerel. Remove the skin and bones and separate the meat into large flakes (Fig. 1). Julienne the shiso.

2. Combine the vinegar, sugar, and salt. Pour over the rice (Fig. 2) and stir quickly.

3. Fold the horse mackerel, shiso, and sesame seeds into the rice.

Sweet Marinated Pumpkin

1¹/₂ oz (40 g) pumpkin • 1 Tbsp vinegar • 1 tsp sugar • Salt • 1 Tbsp water

Slice the pumpkin into matchsticks. Blanch until almost tender. Marinate in the remaining ingredients.

★Place the Mixed Sushi into the container. Add the pumpkin and Stewed Liver (p. 61).
Garnish with a cherry tomato.

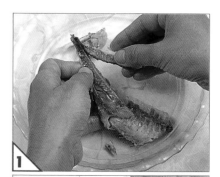

Shrimp and Chrysanthemum Medley

8 shrimp
¹/₂ Japanese cucumber
1 bunch chrysanthemum flowers
1 Tbsp vinegar plus a splash for boiling
¹/₂ tsp sugar
Salt
9 oz (250 g) hot cooked rice

1. Peel, devein, and butterfly the shrimp. Slice the cucumber into thin rounds, sprinkle with salt, knead gently, and squeeze out the liquid. Separate the petals of the chrysanthemum flowers. Drop petals in boiling water with a splash of vinegar. Drain. Marinate in the vinegar, sugar, and salt. Drain well (Fig. 1).

2. Fold the shrimp, cucumber, and chrysanthemum petals into the rice (Fig. 2).

Braised Tofu and Carrot

1 piece freeze-dried tofu, soaked in warm water and well rinsed • 1" (3 cm) carrot, peeled • ²/₃ oz (20 g) string beans • ¹/₂ cup dashi stock • 1 Tbsp mirin • 2 tsp sugar • Salt

1. Gently squeeze out the water from the tofu. Chop the carrot into 6 pieces and smooth the edges. Blanch the string beans and chop.

2. Cook the tofu and carrot in the remaining ingredients for 15 minutes. Add the string beans and cook for 1

minute more. Slice the tofu into bite-sized pieces.

★Try nasturtium or other edible flowers in place of the chrysanthemum. To serve, place the braised vegetables alongside the medley.

Daikon Rice

1" (3 cm) daikon
1/2 Tbsp soy sauce
9 oz (250 g) cooked rice
1/2 package (2.5 g) bonito flakes

1. Cut the daikon into 1/2" (1 cm) dice. Marinate in the soy sauce for 10 minutes (Fig. 1). Drain and pat dry.

2. Stir in the bonito flakes (Fig. 2). Stir the daikon mixture into the rice.

Braised Mackerel

1/2 piece mackerel • 1 piece ginger • 11/2 Tbsp soy sauce • 2 tsp each sugar, mirin, and sake • 3 Tbsp water

1. Cut the mackerel at an angle into 1" (3 cm) strips. Julienne the ginger.

2. Bring all the other ingredients to a boil. Add the mackerel and ginger and cook over high heat for 4–5 minutes.

Japanese Omelets

1 egg, beaten • 1 tsp sake • 1/2 Tbsp sugar • Salt • Cooking oil

1. Stir the sake, sugar, and salt into the egg.

2. In a square pan, make an omelet with the egg mixture. Slice.

Lotus Root Kinpira

1 oz (30 g) lotus root • 1 tsp cooking oil • 1/2 Tbsp soy sauce • 1 tsp each sugar, mirin, and sake • 1 Tbsp water

1. Peel the lotus root and cut lengthwise. Slice into thin half rounds. Soak in cold water. Drain well.

2. Sauté the lotus root in the oil. Add the other ingredients and cook for 2–3 minutes.

★ Pack the Daikon Rice and place the other items alongside. Garnish with blanched snow peas.

RICE MEDLEYS

Rice Medleys are the easiest form of bento. All the ingredients are simply mixed with the cooked rice. To maximize the flavor, be sure the rice is still hot when adding the other ingredients. Leftover rice may be reheated in a microwave or steamer.

Shirasu Rice Medley

1 Tbsp shirasu (dried young sardines) • ¹/₂ piece roasted seaweed • 1 Tbsp roasted sesame seeds • 2 tsp soy sauce • 9 oz (250 g) hot cooked rice

1. Pour boiling water over the shirasu. Drain well. Shred the seaweed.

2. Fold all ingredients into the rice.

Wasabi Fish Cake Medley

1 oz (30 g) fish cake (kamaboko) • 1 tsp fresh wasabi, minced • ¹/₂ tsp each light soy sauce, sake, and salt • 9 oz (250 g) hot cooked rice

1. Cut the fish cake into small dice. Combine with the wasabi, soy sauce, sake, and salt.

2. Fold the fish-cake mixture into the hot rice.

Shrimp and Pickle Medley

1¹/₂ oz (40 g) takanazuke pickles (pickled greens; see p. 40) • 1 Tbsp dried shrimp (sakura-ebi) • 1 tsp cooking oil • 1 tsp each light soy sauce and sake • 9 oz (250 g) hot cooked rice

1. Soak the takanazuke in cold water to remove excess salt. Mince well and squeeze out the water.

2. Sauté the shrimp in a frying pan with the oil. Stir in the takanazuke. Taste the mixture; add the soy sauce and sake gradually.

3. Fold the takanazuke mixture into the hot rice.

Three-Mushroom Rice

(For multiple servings)

2 cups (360 cc) uncooked rice
2 oz (50 g) shimeji mushrooms
4 oz (100 g) enoki mushrooms
4 fresh shiitake mushrooms
1 aburage (tofu puff)
2 Tbsp soy sauce
1 Tbsp sake
1/2 Tbsp mirin
Salt

1. Rinse the rice and drain.
2. Separate the stalks of the shimeji. Cut off the root base of the enoki and chop. Thinly slice the shiitake. Rinse the aburage with boiling water, then julienne.
3. Put the rice in a rice cooker and add the soy sauce, sake, mirin, and salt. Add water to the 2-cup level. Add the ingredients from step 2 (Figure). Start the rice cooker. When done, gently fold the mushrooms into the cooked rice.

Seafood Omelet

1 egg, beaten • 2 Tbsp dried shirasu • Chives, minced • 1/2 Tbsp sugar • 1 tsp sake • Salt • Cooking oil

1. Stir the shirasu, chives, sugar, sake, and salt into the egg.
2. Cook the egg mixture in the oil, forming a small omelet.

Spicy Konnyaku
1/3 piece konnyaku (devil's-tongue jelly) • 1/2 cup dashi stock • 2 tsp soy sauce • 1 tsp mirin • 1 tsp sake • Shichimi-togarashi (7-spice powder)

Tear the konnyaku into small pieces. Parboil. Simmer in the liquid ingredients until all fluid has evaporated. Sprinkle with the shichimi-togarashi.

Miso-Filled Peppers
4 sweet peppers • 3 Tbsp miso • Cooking oil

Make a vertical slit in each sweet pepper and spoon the miso inside. Cook the pepper packets over high heat in the oil until lightly browned.

★Use a lettuce leaf to separate the items. Garnish with apple slices.

Sweet-Potato Rice

(For multiple servings)

2 cups (360 cc) uncooked rice
1 small sweet potato (7 oz; 200 g)
2 tsp sake
3/4 tsp salt

1. Rinse the rice and drain.

2. Wash the sweet potato. Cut into 1/2" (1 cm) dice. Soak in cold water, then drain.

3. Put the rice in a rice cooker and add the sake and salt. Add water to the 2-cup level. Add the sweet potatoes (Fig. 1) and start the rice cooker.

4. When done, check that the potatoes are well steamed (Fig. 2). (If not, replace the cover and let stand another 5 minutes.) Stir the potatoes into the rice.

Mackerel Teriyaki

1 piece Spanish mackerel (sawara) • Salt and pepper • Pastry flour for dredging • Cooking oil • 1/2 Tbsp soy sauce • 1 tsp sake • 1 tsp mirin

1. Slice the mackerel at an angle. Sprinkle with salt and pepper and dredge in the flour.

2. Heat the oil in a frying pan. Cook the mackerel briefly on all sides. Add the other ingredients and cook over high heat until well glazed.

Cauliflower-Cucumber Pickles

1/2 Japanese cucumber • Salt • 1 1/2 oz (40 g) cauliflower florets • 1 tsp citron juice • 2 tsp vinegar • 1/2 tsp sugar • 2 slices citron zest

1. Slice the cucumber into thin rounds. Sprinkle with salt, knead gently, and squeeze out the water. Boil the cauliflower until just tender.

2. Toss the cauliflower and cucumber with the remaining ingredients.

★Garnish with citron zest and narazuke (daikon pickled in a soy-miso-sake mixture).

Savory Tofu Rice

(For multiple servings)

2 cups (360 cc) uncooked rice
1 yard (1 m) kampyo (dried gourd
   strips)
Salt
1/2 piece freeze-dried tofu
2 dried shiitake mushrooms,
   soaked in cold water
1" (3 cm) carrot
2/3 cup dashi stock
21/2 Tbsp soy sauce
2 tsp sugar
1 Tbsp each mirin and sake

1. Wash and drain the rice.
2. Rub the kampyo with salt to soften,
then parboil and chop. Soak the freeze-
dried tofu in warm water and squeeze
out the water. Cut the tofu, shiitake, and
carrots into 3/8" (8 mm) dice.
3. Heat the remaining ingredients in a
pot. Add the tofu mixture and cook 7–8
minutes (Fig. 1). Drain and set aside,
reserving liquid.
4. Put the rice in a rice cooker. Add the
liquid from step 3 (Fig. 2) plus enough
water to reach the 2-cup level. Start the
rice cooker.
5. When the rice is ready, put the tofu
mixture on top and close the cooker. Let
stand for 10 minutes to steam. Gently
fold the mixture into the rice.

Ginger Beef

3 oz (80 g) thinly sliced beef, cut into
strips • 11/2" (4 cm) takuan (yellow daikon
pickles), cut into strips • 1 Tbsp cooking
oil • 2 green shiso leaves, julienned • 2
tsp soy sauce • 1 tsp sake • 1/2 tsp juice
from grated ginger

1. Sauté the beef and takuan in the oil.
2. Combine the soy sauce, sake, and
ginger juice and stir into the pan.
Sprinkle with the shiso.

Spinach Rolls

1 oz (30 g) spinach • 1/2 beaten egg • Salt
• Cooking oil

1. Blanch the spinach in salted water.
Plunge in cold water and gently squeeze
out the liquid. Stir salt into the egg and
make a thin omelet with the cooking oil.
2. Place the omelet on a sushi mat. Put
the spinach in the center and roll tightly.
Cut the roll into three pieces.

★Place the Spinach Rolls and Ginger
Beef alongside the Savory Tofu Rice.
Garnish with Tora Mame (p. 59).

THREE RICE CASSEROLES

Water quantity is the key for perfect rice casseroles. Even though the added ingredients add volume, the water usually goes no higher than the normal level in the rice cooker. *(These three recipes are for multiple servings.)*

Sushi Casserole

2 cups (360 cc) uncooked rice • 4 oz (100 g) crabmeat • 2 oz (50 g) boiled bamboo shoot • 2 oz (50 g) shimeji mushrooms • 1 aburage (tofu puff) • $3^{1}/_{2}$ Tbsp vinegar • $1^{1}/_{3}$ Tbsp sugar • $^{2}/_{3}$ tsp salt

1. Wash and drain the rice.

2. Separate the crabmeat into large pieces. Cut the bamboo shoots into thin rectangles. Clean the shimeji and divide the stalks. Rinse the aburage in boiling water and julienne.

3. Put the rice in a rice cooker and add the vinegar, sugar, and salt. Add water to reach the normal level. Place the other ingredients on top. Start the rice cooker.

4. Let the rice cooker stand for 10 minutes after cooking. Gently fold the ingredients into the rice.

Chicken and Gobo Casserole

2 cups (360 cc) uncooked rice • 4 oz (100 g) chicken thigh meat, minced • 4 oz (100 g) gobo (burdock root) • Small piece of carrot • $2^{2}/_{3}$ Tbsp soy sauce • 1 Tbsp sake • 2 tsp sugar • 2 tsp mirin

1. Wash and drain the rice.

2. Using a vegetable peeler, cut the gobo into thin, short strips. Blanch. Julienne the carrots.

3. Follow steps 3 and 4 as for the Sushi Casserole.

Taro and Daikon Casserole

2 cups (360 cc) uncooked rice • 2 taro roots • 2" (5 cm) daikon • 2 Tbsp young sardines (chirimenjako) • 2 Tbsp miso • 2 Tbsp sake

1. Wash and drain the rice.

2. Slice the taro into quarter rounds. Cut the daikon into matchsticks 1" (2.5 cm) long and $^{1}/_{4}$" (5 mm) thick. Dry-roast the young sardines in a frying pan and set aside. Combine the miso and sake.

3. Put the rice and miso mixture in a rice cooker. Add water to slightly less than 2-cup level. Place the taro and daikon on top. Start the cooker.

4. Let the rice cooker stand for 10 minutes after cooking. Fold the taro and daikon into the rice and add the young sardines.

Tempura Rice Triangles

10 oz (300 g) hot cooked rice

3 prawns

1½ Tbsp pastry flour plus more
   for dredging

1 quail's egg

1 Tbsp water

1 Tbsp Dipping Sauce (p. 47)

Roasted seaweed

Oil for deep-frying

1. Devein the prawns. Peel, leaving the tail on. Cut the vein on the inside and flatten out the prawn.

2. Combine the flour with the beaten quail egg and water to form a batter. Dredge the prawns lightly in additional flour, then dip in the batter. Deep fry at 350° F (175° C).

3. Form the rice into three balls. Dip each prawn into the warmed sauce and then press it into the center of the ball (Fig. 1). Shape the ball into a triangle. Wrap with a strip of seaweed (Fig. 2).

Soy Turnip

1 turnip with leaves • 1 tsp soy sauce

Remove the turnip leaves and reserve (see below), leaving ½" of stem. Peel the turnip and cut into wedges. Toss with the soy sauce.

Turnip Leaves and Enoki Sauté

Leaves from 1 turnip • 1 oz (30 g) enoki mushrooms • 1 tsp cooking oil • Salt and pepper

1. Boil the turnip leaves in salted water until almost tender and chop. Remove the base of the enoki and chop.

2. Sauté the enoki and turnip leaves in the oil. Season with salt and pepper.

Savory Simmered Beef

2 oz (60 g) beef, sliced paper thin • Ginger, julienned • 1 tsp each mirin, sake, and sugar • 1 Tbsp soy sauce • 2 Tbsp water

1. Cut the beef into strips.

2. Bring the remaining ingredients to a boil. Add the beef. Cook, stirring, for 3 minutes.

★For paper-thin beef, ask for sukiyaki meat at Japanese specialty stores. To serve, arrange the rice triangles with the other items. Garnish with orange wedges.

Roasted Rice Balls

14 oz (400 g) hot cooked rice
2 tsp miso
1 tsp sake
2 tsp soy sauce

1. Form the rice into four balls. Combine the miso with *¹/₂ tsp* of the sake and set aside. Combine the soy sauce with the remaining sake and set aside.
2. Grill or broil the rice balls on both sides (Fig. 1).
3. Brush two of the rice balls with the miso mixture and brush the other two with the soy sauce mixture. Continue grilling or broiling until well browned.

Chicken Teriyaki Rolls

4 oz (100 g) chicken thigh, with skin •
Cooking oil • 2 tsp soy sauce • 1 tsp mirin
• 1 tsp sake • ¹/₂ tsp sugar • 3 Tbsp water

1. Cut into the thickest part of the thigh and flatten out the meat, skin side down. Roll up into a small, even cylinder. Tie loosely with kitchen string.
2. Cook the chicken roll in the oil until browned on all sides. Add the remaining ingredients and cook, turning, until well glazed. Slice into diagonal rounds.

Miso-Infused Asparagus

2 spears asparagus, trimmed • ¹/₂ Tbsp
miso • 1 tsp vinegar • 1 tsp sugar • ¹/₂
tsp Asian hot mustard • Salt

1. Boil asparagus in salted water and chop.
2. Combine the remaining ingredients and toss with the asparagus.

Grilled Fish Cakes and Shiitake

3 slices (¹/₄"; 5 mm) kamaboko (fish cake)
• 1 fresh shiitake mushroom • Soy sauce

1. Make a lengthwise slit in the center of each kamaboko slice. Pull one end of the kamaboko through the slit to make an elegant twist shape. Grill or broil until lightly browned.
2. Grill or broil the shiitake until browned. Drizzle soy sauce on the shiitake and slice.

★ Tuck all the items next to the Rice Balls.

RICE BALL WRAPPINGS

**Here are six unique rice-ball wrapping methods.
Fillings can be varied, too, to make endless new combinations.**

Konbu Sheets

Wrap the entire ball in sheets of tororo konbu. Warm rice softens the konbu and helps it stay in place.

Egg Crepe

Cook 1 beaten egg with a little oil in a large skillet as if to make a crepe. Let cool, then wrap around the rice ball to make a cheerful yellow package.

Pickled Greens

The saltiness of takanazuke (pickled greens) blends beautifully with rice balls. Mince the stems and mix with the rice before rolling. Use the leaves to wrap the rice balls.

Rice Crackers

These miniature rice crackers are usually used for ochazuke (hot tea poured over rice). See p. 20 for another use of the crackers.

Cod Roe Sprinkles

Roll the warm rice ball in a plate of Cod Roe Sprinkles (p. 63). The roe adheres better to warm rice.

Green Sesame Sprinkles

Coat the rice ball in Turnip-Leaf Sprinkles (p. 63). Keep the sprinkles handy for a quick treat.

How to Make Rice Balls

To make delicious rice balls every time, use rice that is still warm and press gently but firmly.

To prevent the rice from sticking, have a bowl of salted cold water ready. Put some of the salt water in the palm of your hand before picking up the rice. Each rice ball should be small enough to fit easily in one hand.

Disk	**Triangle**	**Capsule**

1. Cup your left hand to create the rounded edge. Press gently, turning, with your right hand.

1. Form the bottom with your left hand and the top corner with your right hand.

1. Form the cylinder with your right hand while turning in your left hand.

2. To finish, curve your right thumb and finger around the ball. Use your left hand to regulate the thickness.

2. Pressing the triangle into the palm of your left hand, squeeze each corner of the triangle with your right hand.

2. Holding the cylinder in your left hand, press the top and bottom into shape with your right thumb and fingers.

Fried Rice

1 oz (30 g) thinly sliced beef

1 egg, beaten

1½ Tbsp cooking oil

2" (5 cm) naganegi (Japanese bunching onion)

Salt and pepper

10 oz (300 g) hot cooked rice

2 tsp soy sauce

1 tsp sake

1. Cut the beef into strips. Stir a pinch of *salt* into the beaten egg. Chop naganegi coarsely.

2. Sauté the meat and naganegi in *½ Tbsp* of the oil. Season with salt and pepper and remove from pan (Fig. 1).

3. Add the remaining oil to the pan and scramble the egg.

4. Add the rice to the pan and stir fry, breaking up the egg. Stir in the meat mixture (Fig.2). Add the soy sauce and sake.

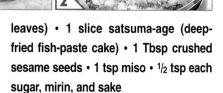

Seasoned Tofu

2 small ganmodoki (deep-fried tofu-vegetable cubes) • ½ cup dashi stock • ½ Tbsp mirin • ½ Tbsp sake • 2 tsp soy sauce • 2 tsp sugar

Rinse the ganmodoki with boiling water. Bring all other ingredients to a boil, then add ganmodoki. Cook until all liquid has been absorbed. Cut into bite-sized pieces.

Sesame-Miso Greens

3 oz (80 g) shungiku (chrysanthemum leaves) • 1 slice satsuma-age (deep-fried fish-paste cake) • 1 Tbsp crushed sesame seeds • 1 tsp miso • ½ tsp each sugar, mirin, and sake

1. Blanch the shungiku and plunge in cold water. Squeeze out the liquid and chop. Cut the satsuma-age into matchsticks.

2. Combine the remaining ingredients into a paste, then toss with the shungiku and satsuma-age.

★Pack the Fried Rice and other items in the container. Garnish with a banana slice.

THREE FRIED RICE VARIETIES

Try these tasty fried-rice recipes, each infused with uniquely Japanese flavors.

Shrimp Rice

2–3 pieces tree-ear fungus • 2 Tbsp dried shrimp (sakura-ebi) • 1 Tbsp cooking oil • 9 oz (250 g) hot cooked rice • 2 tsp soy sauce • 2 tsp sake • 3 green shiso leaves, julienned

1. Soak the fungus in cold water and julienne.

2. Sauté the fungus and shrimp in the oil. Add the rice to the pan and stir fry.

3. Add the soy sauce and sake. Remove from heat and stir in the shiso.

Salmon-Cucumber Rice

2½ oz (70 g) canned salmon • ½ Japanese cucumber • Minced ginger • 1 Tbsp cooking oil • 9 oz (250 g) hot cooked rice • ½ tsp salt • Pepper

1. Drain the salmon and separate into flakes. Chop the cucumber.

2. Sauté the salmon, cucumber, and ginger briefly in *½ Tbsp* of the oil, then remove from the pan.

3. Add the remaining oil to the pan and sauté the rice. Return the salmon mixture to the pan and season with salt and pepper.

Miso-Pickle Rice

2" (5 cm) misozuke yamagobo (wild burdock root pickled with miso) • 2" (5 cm) celery • 2 oz (50 g) boneless skinless chicken breast, chopped • 1 Tbsp cooking oil • Celery leaves, julienned • 9 oz (250 g) hot cooked rice • Salt and pepper

1. Slice the misozuke into thin rounds. Remove the strings of the celery, cut in half lengthwise, and chop into ¼"-thick (5 mm) pieces.

2. Sauté the chicken in the oil. Season with salt and pepper. Stir in the celery, then the misozuke, and then the celery leaves. Add the rice and stir until combined. Correct the seasonings.

Tricolor Rice

Salmon Sprinkles

1 piece fresh salmon
1¹/₂ Tbsp sugar
1 tsp each mirin and sake
¹/₃ tsp salt
2 Tbsp water

1. Boil the salmon for 3–4 minutes until cooked through. Drain.

2. Removing any skin or bones, gently crush the salmon in a mortar.

3. Put the salmon in a pot and add the remaining ingredients (Fig. 1). Turn on the flame. Stirring continuously with 3–5 chopsticks, cook until all liquid has been absorbed (Fig. 2).

Egg Sprinkles

1 egg, beaten • 1 Tbsp sugar • Cooking oil • Salt

Stir the sugar and salt into the egg. Cook over high heat in the oil, stirring well, until egg separates into tiny bits.

Spinach Sauté

2 oz (50 g) spinach • Cooking oil • Salt

Blanch the spinach in salted water. Squeeze out the water and mince. Sauté briefly in the oil and season with salt.

Glazed Chicken Wings

2 chicken wings • 1 tsp cooking oil • 2 tsp soy sauce • 1 tsp sake • 1 tsp mirin •

²/₃ tsp sugar

1. Cut each wing into two pieces at the joint. Score the meat along the bone.

2. Sauté the wing pieces in the oil until browned. Add *1/2 cup water* and cook for 10 minutes. Add the remaining ingredients and cook, stirring, until the wings are well glazed.

★Arrange the salmon sprinkles, egg sprinkles, and spinach sauté in a decorative pattern atop the rice. Add the chicken wings and garnish with sliced strawberries.

COLORFUL SPRINKLES

(All four of these recipes are for multiple servings.)

Sprinkles keep in the refrigerator for up to a week and make a delicious combination with any of the side items in this book.

Cod Sprinkles

Shrimp Sprinkles

1 piece sweet salted cod • 1 slice lemon • 1½ Tbsp sugar • 1 Tbsp sake • 2 Tbsp water • Salt

1. Cook the cod and lemon slice in boiling water for 3 minutes, then drain. Remove the skin and bones and the lemon, then gently crush in a mortar.

2. Place in a pot with the remaining ingredients. Bring to a boil. Stir with 3−5 chopsticks until the liquid is absorbed and the sprinkles are dry.

4 oz (100 g) shrimp, peeled and deveined • 1 Tbsp each sugar, mirin and sake • 1 Tbsp water • Salt

1. Boil the shrimp, drain, and mince.

2. Put the shrimp in a pot with the remaining ingredients. Bring to a boil. Stir with 3−5 chopsticks until the liquid is absorbed.

Chicken Sprinkles

Horse Mackerel Sprinkles

3½ Tbsp soy sauce • 1½ Tbsp sugar • 2 Tbsp mirin • 2 Tbsp sake • 2 Tbsp water • 7 oz (200 g) ground chicken • 1 piece ginger, minced

1. Bring the first five ingredients to a boil. Add the chicken and ginger.

2. Stirring with 3−5 chopsticks, cook until the sprinkles are nearly dry.

1 horse mackerel (aji) • Julienned ginger • 1 Tbsp soy sauce • ½Tbsp mirin • ½ Tbsp sake • 2 Tbsp water • Pinch salt

1. Clean the horse mackerel, season with the salt, and broil. Remove the skin and bones and gently crush in a mortar.

2. Place in a pot with the remaining ingredients. Bring to a boil. Stirring with 3−5 chopsticks, cook until the liquid is absorbed.

Yaki Udon

1 oz (30 g) shimeji mushrooms
4" (10 cm) naganegi (Japanese bunching onion)
1 oz (30 g) thinly sliced pork, in strips
1 Tbsp cooking oil
Salt and pepper
1 portion cooked udon
1 Tbsp each soy sauce and sake

1. Separate the shimeji into stalks. Cut the naganegi into diagonal slices.

2. Sauté the pork, naganegi, and shimeji in *1 tsp* of the oil (Fig. 1). Season lightly with salt and pepper and remove from pan.

3. Add the remaining oil to the pan and sauté the udon gently, separating the strands (Fig. 2). Stir in the pork mixture. Add the soy sauce and sake.

Swordfish Fingers

1½ oz (40 g) swordfish • 1 tsp cooking oil • ½ Tbsp each soy sauce, mirin, and sake • ½ Tbsp water • Roasted seaweed

1. Slice the swordfish into ³/₈"-thick (1 cm) strips. Sauté in the oil.

2. Add the liquid ingredients and bring to a boil. Cook the swordfish until well glazed. Remove from pan and wrap their centers with strips of seaweed.

Orange-Cabbage Salad

2 pieces Chinese cabbage, julienned • ½ fresh mandarin orange • 1 Tbsp vinegar • 1 Tbsp cooking oil • Salt and pepper

1. Salt the Chinese cabbage, knead gently, and squeeze out the liquid. Remove the membranes from the orange sections.

2. Combine the remaining ingredients. Toss with the orange sections and Chinese cabbage.

★Put the Yaki Udon in the container. Place the Swordfish Fingers atop a piece of lettuce. The Orange-Cabbage Salad goes in a separate container.

NOODLES GALORE

Use these refreshing noodle bento combinations for a change of pace from rice-based bento.

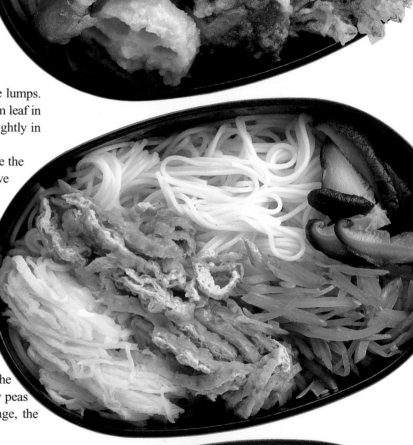

Tempura Soba

2 prawns • 1 sweet pepper • 2 Tbsp pastry flour • 1 Tbsp beaten egg • 1/2 Tbsp water • 1 fresh shiitake mushroom • 3/8" (1 cm) lotus root • 1 chrysanthemum leaf (shungiku) • Oil for deep-frying • 4 oz (100 g) dry soba noodles
Dipping Sauce < 1/2 cup dashi stock • 2 Tbsp mirin • 2 Tbsp soy sauce >

1. Peel the prawns, leaving tails on, devein, and butterfly. Make vertical slits in the sweet pepper.

2. Combine the flour, egg, and water quickly, leaving some lumps. Dip the sweet pepper, shiitake, lotus root, and chrysanthemum leaf in the batter and fry at 340° F (170° C). Dredge the shrimp lightly in the flour and dip in the batter, then fry.

3. Boil the soba until almost tender and drain well. Combine the sauce ingredients and bring to a boil in a separate pan. Remove from heat.

4. Place the soba in the container and top with the tempura. Put the dipping sauce in a separate container.

Somen Deluxe

1 egg • 3 tsp sugar • Salt • Cooking oil • 1 aburage (tofu puff) • 2 tsp each mirin, soy sauce, and sake • 4 Tbsp water • 5 snow peas • Sweet Simmered Shiitake (p. 59) • 4 oz (100 g) dry somen noodles
Dipping Sauce (same as Tempura Soba above)

1. Beat the egg with *1 tsp* of the sugar and a pinch of salt. Heat the oil and make a thin omelet. Boil the aburage with the liquid ingredi-ents and the remaining sugar. String the snow peas and blanch in salted water. Julienne the omelet, the aburage, the snow peas, and the shiitake.

2. Boil the somen and set as same as the step 4 of Tempura Soba.

Somen Stir Fry

1 chicken breast tenderloin • 1/2 green pepper • 1/4 carrot, julienned • 4 oz (100 g) somen • 2 tsp cooking oil • 1 tsp sake • 1/2 tsp soy sauce • 1/3 tsp salt • Red pepper flakes (ichimi-togarashi) to taste

1. Trim the chicken and cut into strips. Slice the green pepper into paper-thin rounds. Boil the somen until almost tender and drain well.

2. Stir-fry the chicken and vegetables in the oil. Stir in the somen. Add the sake, soy sauce, and salt, and sprinkle with the red pepper flakes.

LOW-FAT TEMPTATIONS

Though most Japanese food is already low in calories, these delectable combinations use extra low-fat ingredients and cooking methods.

Spanish Mackerel Teriyaki

2/3 piece Spanish mackerel
  (sawara)
2 tsp soy sauce
1 tsp each mirin and sake
1/2 tsp cornstarch

1. Slice the sawara at an angle. Marinate in the liquid ingredients for 10 minutes (Fig 1, facing page).
2. Drain, reserving marinade. Place on a rack, and grill or broil on both sides.
3. Add *1 Tbsp water* to the marinade and bring to a boil. Blend the cornstarch with *1 tsp water* and add to the pan. Cook until thickened. Brush the sauce on the sawara (Fig. 2) and grill or broil a little longer.

Golden Daikon

1/2 aburage (tofu puff) • 2 oz (50 g) daikon, julienned • 1/2 Tbsp cooking oil • 2 Tbsp dashi stock • 2 tsp soy sauce • 2 tsp sake • 1 tsp mirin

1. Rinse the aburage in boiling water and julienne.
2. Sauté the daikon and aburage in the oil. Add the remaining ingredients and cook until the liquid is almost absorbed.

Fish Cake and Cucumber in Wasabi

1" (3 cm) kamaboko (fish cake) • 1/2 Japanese cucumber • 1 tsp wasabi-zuke (wasabi pickles) • Salt

1. Thinly slice the kamaboko. Cut the cucumber into 1"-long (3 cm) thin rectangles. Sprinkle with the salt, knead gently, and squeeze out the liquid.
2. Combine all ingredients.

★Place the Spanish Mackerel Teriyaki on top of the rice. Add the rest of the items.

Snapper and Mushrooms en Papillote

1 small snapper fillet
1 tsp sake
1/4 tsp salt
1 oz (30 g) shimeji mushrooms,
  in stalks
Chives, chopped

1. Cut the fillet into bite-sized pieces. Marinate in the salt and sake (Fig. 1).
2. Place the snapper and shimeji on parchment paper (Fig. 2) and wrap. Twist the ends to seal.
3. Bake 3–4 minutes in a toaster oven or under the broiler. Open the paper from the top and sprinkle the chives inside.

Toaster-Poached Egg

1 egg • Soy sauce

Crack an egg into an aluminum-foil cup (see illustration, opposite page). Cook in a toaster oven for 3–4 minutes or until firm. Drizzle soy sauce on top.

Stir-Fried Wakame

1/3 oz (10 g) salted dried wakame • 1/2 tsp cooking oil • 1/2 Tbsp sake • 1/2 tsp light soy sauce

Soak the wakame in cold water, then drain well. Chop coarsely and stir-fry in the oil. Add the sake and soy sauce.

★Place the Stir-Fried Wakame and some takuan (yellow daikon pickles) on the rice.The fish package and the egg in its cup go right into the container.

Tofu Dumplings

2 oz (50 g) ground chicken
2 oz (50 g) firm tofu, well drained
1 quail's egg, beaten
Naganegi (Japanese bunching onion), minced
1 Tbsp pastry flour
Salt and pepper
2 tsp soy sauce
1 tsp each mirin and sake
1/2 tsp sugar
3 Tbsp water
1/2 tsp cornstarch

1. Crush the chicken well in a mortar. Add the tofu, quail egg, flour, salt, pepper, and naganegi and continue crush-ing until well blended (Fig. 1).

2. Using a wet teaspoon, drop spoonfuls of the tofu mixture into boiling water. Simmer until they rise to the top of the water (Fig. 2).

3. Bring the remaining 5 ingredients to a boil in another pan. Add the dump-lings and boil for 2–3 minutes. Blend the cornstarch with *1 tsp water* and stir into the pan until the sauce is thickened.

Lemon-Infused Crab Salad

1 oz (30 g) cooked crabmeat • 1 1/3 oz (40 g) daikon • 1" (3 cm) Japanese cucumber • 2 tsp lemon juice • Salt

1. Pull the crab pieces apart into chunks. Cut the daikon and cucumber into thin rectangles, sprinkle with salt, knead gen-tly, and squeeze out the liquid.

2. Combine all ingredients with the lemon juice.

★Cut seaweed into squares and dip in soy sauce, then place on the rice in a checkerboard pattern. Use butter lettuce to separate the Tofu Dumplings from the salad.

Chicken Medallions

2 chicken breast tenderloins
1 tsp sake
Salt
Pastry flour for dredging
1 beaten egg
Cooking oil

1. Trim the tenderloins and pound until thin. Cut at an angle into large pieces and sprinkle with the sake and salt. Pat dry. Dredge each piece lightly in the flour and dip in the egg (Fig. 1) (Reserve the remaining egg.)

2. Cook the chicken in the oil (Fig. 2) until browned on both sides. Lower the heat and continue cooking until the chicken is no longer pink inside, then remove from the pan.

3. Dip the cooked chicken pieces in the egg a second time and cook again until the egg coating is golden brown.

Stewed Gobo

2 oz (50 g) gobo (burdock root) • ¹/₃ cup dashi stock • 2 tsp soy sauce • 1 tsp mirin • 1 tsp sake • 2 tsp sugar • Bonito flakes

1. Scrape the skin off of the gobo. Slice diagonally into ¹/₈"-thick (3 mm) ovals. Blanch, rinse in cold water, and drain.

2. Bring all remaining ingredients except the bonito to a boil. Add the gobo and lower the heat, simmering until the liquid is almost all absorbed.

3. Stir in the bonito and heat briefly.

Braised Konbu

2 oz (50 g) kiri-konbu (julienned konbu) • ¹/₂ stick chikuwa (fish-cake tube) • ¹/₂ Tbsp cooking oil • ¹/₂ Tbsp light soy sauce • ¹/₂ Tbsp sake • 2 Tbsp water

1. Chop the konbu coarsely. Julienne the chikuwa lengthwise.

2. Sauté the konbu and chikuwa in the oil. Add the liquid ingredients and bring to a boil.

★Place the Chicken Medallions on the rice. The other items go alongside.

SPECIAL CREATIONS

For important occasions, try these elegant combinations.
They are breathtaking when served in *ojubako*—stacked lacquered lunch boxes.

Five-Color Sushi Bowl *(For multiple servings)*

2 cups (360 cc) uncooked rice
1 freeze-dried tofu, soaked in
   warm water
1 yard (1 m) dried gourd strips
   (kampyo)
1 aburage (tofu puff)
1½" (4 cm) carrot
½ cup dashi stock
2½ Tbsp soy sauce
2½ Tbsp sugar
½ Tbsp each mirin and sake
1½ tsp salt
3 pieces Sweet Simmered Shiitake (p. 59), julienned
1 oz (30 g) lotus root
4 Tbsp vinegar
1 Tbsp water
½ beaten egg
Cooking oil
2–3 snow peas

1. Rinse and drain the rice.
2. Squeeze out the water from the freeze-dried tofu and julienne. Soak the gourd in warm water, rub with salt, boil, and cut into ³/₈" (1 cm) lengths. Rinse the aburage in boiling water and julienne. Julienne the carrot.
3. Simmer all the ingredients from step 2 in the stock, soy sauce, mirin, sake, and ½ *Tbsp* of the sugar until the liquid has evaporated. Toss in the shiitake.
4. Cook the rice with water to slightly lower than the 2-cup level. While the rice cooks, combine 1½ *Tbsp* of the sugar with 3 *Tbsp* of the vinegar and ²/₃ *tsp* of the salt. Pour the vinegar mixture over the hot cooked rice (Fig. 1), stirring in with a cutting motion.
5. Incorporate the ingredients from step 3 into the rice (Fig. 2).
6. Slice the lotus root into thin rounds. Cook with the water and the remaining vinegar, *1 tsp* of the sugar, and salt until the liquid has evaporated.
7. Stir a pinch of salt and sugar into the egg. Cook with the oil to make a thin omelet. Remove from heat and julienne. String the snow peas, blanch in salted water, and julienne.
8. Put the rice mixture into the container. Sprinkle with the lotus root, egg strips, and snow peas.

Braised Pork
(For multiple servings)

10 oz (300 g) pork loin • 1 Tbsp cooking oil • Ginger, sliced thin • Naganegi (Japanese bunching onion), chopped • 3 Tbsp soy sauce • 1 Tbsp mirin • 1 Tbsp sake • 2 tsp sugar

1. Pierce the pork all over with a fork. Brown well in the oil.
2. Add the ginger and naganegi, then add water just to cover. Bring to a boil, then simmer over lower heat for 20 minutes.
3. Add the remaining ingredients and continue cooking until the sauce has reduced.

★Blanch 2–3 asparagus spears in salted water. Cut into pieces and stir into the sauce. Place the pork slice in the container with the asparagus next to it, then pour the remaining sauce on top.

Grilled Cuttlefish

¼ piece of large cuttlefish steak • ½ Tbsp neri-uni (sea urchin paste) • 1 tsp sake

1. Peel the cuttlefish. Score in a criss-cross pattern. Broil on a rack.
2. Combine the other two ingredients and brush on the cuttlefish. Continue broiling until the glaze is golden brown.

Hanpen Soup

¼ piece hanpen • Soy sauce • ¾ package ochazuke mix

1. Place the hanpen on a rack and broil, brushing with soy sauce. Cut into ³/₈"- (8 mm) dice.
2. Put the hanpen and ochazuke mix into a bowl. Pour boiling water over.

★When ready to serve, transfer the hanpen mixture to a soup bowl and add boiling water.

Makunouchi

Chicken Rolls

(For multiple servings)

2 oz (50 g) ground chicken
2 eggs, beaten
1 Tbsp grated onion
2 Tbsp breadcrumbs
Salt
2–3 string beans
2–3 carrot sticks
(3"-long, 1/4"-thick; 7 cm x 5 mm)
Cooking oil

1. Crush the chicken well in a mortar. Stir in *2 tsp* of the egg, the breadcrumbs, the onion, and a pinch of salt.

2. Blanch the string beans and carrots in salted water.

3. Stir a pinch of salt into the remaining beaten egg. Scramble the egg in the oil until it is set but not dry.

4. Cut a sheet of aluminum foil into a 10" (25 cm) square and place it on a sushi rolling mat. Brush with a small amount of oil. Spread with the chicken mixture, then the egg, then put the carrot and beans in the center. Roll as for sushi.

5. Place in a hot steamer. Cook over high heat for 7–8 minutes. Slice into rounds.

Carrots and Butterbur

1 fuki (butterbur)
1" (3 cm) carrot
1/3 cup dashi stock
1 tsp sugar
1 tsp mirin
Salt

1. Parboil the butterbur in salted water. Peel and cut into 1" (3 cm) lengths, then plunge in cold water. Quarter the carrot lengthwise, peel, and shave off the sharp corners.

2. Simmer the carrots in the dashi stock, sugar, mirin, and salt for 7–8 minutes. Raise the heat, add the butterbur, and boil for 2–3 minutes.

Octopus Tempura

1/2 boiled octopus leg
1 Tbsp pastry flour
1 tsp beaten egg
Aonori (green seaweed sprinkles)
Oil for deep-frying

1. Slice the octopus in diagonal rounds.

2. Combine the flour, egg, and aonori. Dip the octopus in the batter and fry at 350° F (175° C).

Crab-Cucumber Salad

1" (3 cm) Japanese cucumber
1/2 beaten egg
1 tsp sugar
1 Tbsp vinegar
Salt
2/3 oz (20 g) cooked crab

1. Cut the cucumber into rectangles. Sprinkle with salt.

2. Combine the egg with *1/2 tsp* of the sugar and some salt. Scramble the egg, then cool.

3. Combine the vinegar with the remaining sugar and some salt. Toss with the egg, crab, and cucumber.

★Form the rice into cylinders as 'Capsule' on page 41. Sprinkle with black sesame seeds and place in the bento box. Place all the other items in the box, garnishing the simmered vegetables with a small branch of leaves.

Quick Miso Soup

¹/₄ aburage (tofu puff) • Fu (dried wheat gluten) • 1 miso ball ⁽*⁾

1. Grill the aburage and julienne.

2. Put the Miso Ball, fu, and aburage into a bowl. Stir in hot water when ready to serve.

⁽*⁾Miso Ball : Combine 1 Tbsp miso, chopped naganegi, and ¹/₅ package (1 g) bonito flakes and form into a ball. Place on a skewer or fork and roast on all sides over a flame.

Red Bean Rice

(For multiple servings)

2 cups (360 cc) uncooked glutinous rice
¼ cup black-eyed peas (sasage)
⅓ tsp salt

1. Wash and drain the rice.
2. Wash the beans. Add water to cover and bring to boil. Drain (reserve, see next step), add 1 cup fresh water, and simmer 15 minutes (Fig. 1).
3. Add enough water with the salt to the reserved liquid to make a scant 1½ cups (340 cc).
4. Put the rice in a rice cooker. Pour in the liquid of step 3 (Fig. 2) and spoon the beans on top. Turn on the cooker. When done, fold the beansinto the rice.

Steamed Miso Chicken

3 oz (80 g) chicken breast
Sake and salt
2 tsp miso
3–4 brussels sprouts
½ tsp soy sauce
½ tsp sake
Naganegi (Japanese bunching onion), minced
Ginger, minced
½ Tbsp cooking oil

1. Sprinkle sake and salt on chicken. Cook in a microwave oven(*) for 1½ minutes. Slice, reserving liquid.
2. Combine the miso, soy sauce, sake, naganegi, and ginger into the reserved liquid.
3. Cook the brussels sprouts till almost tender. Cut into quarters.

4. Sauté the chicken and brussels sprouts in the oil. Stir in the miso mixture (step 2).

(*)The time listed is for a 500-watt oven.

Salmon Rolls

1½" (4 cm) daikon, peeled
1½" (4 cm) Japanese cucumber
2 pieces smoked salmon
Salt

1. Cut the daikon and cucumber into thin, wide slabs, as if to peel them. Soak in thick salted water until soft. Pat dry.
2. Layer the daikon and cucumber on a sushi mat. Put the salmon in the center and roll up into a cylinder. Cut crosswise into two pieces.

Lily Bulbs

3–4 lily bulbs (edible)
3 Tbsp dashi stock
½ tsp sugar
½ tsp mirin
½ tsp sake
Salt

1. Boil the lily bulbs in warm water for 1–2 minutes. Drain.
2. Cook the bulbs with all other ingredients over low heat until tender.

★Pack the Red Bean Rice in one level of the bento box. Sprinkle with a mixture of salt and parched sesame seeds. Put the other items in another level, with Tricolor Vegetables (p.63). Garnish with sliced mandarin oranges.

Quick Mushroom Soup

⅔ oz (20 g) shimeji mushrooms • ⅔ oz (20 g) enoki mushrooms • 2 Tbsp dashi stock • ½ Tbsp soy sauce • ½ tsp mirin • 1 tsp sake • Scallions, chopped

1. Clean the shimeji and separate the stalks. Cut off the root end of the enoki and chop.
2. Bring the liquid ingredients to a boil and add the mushrooms. Cook, stirring, 2–3 minutes, to make a mushroom syrup. This syrup can be placed in a sealed container. When ready to serve, pour hot water over the syrup and sprinkle with the scallions.

BENTO HELPERS

Keep some of these helpers on hand for quick assembly of a complete bento. All of these staples will keep in the refrigerator for up to a week, and because they are more easily prepared in batches, the proportions have been designed for convenience. Reheat the portions before putting them in the bento.

(All of these recipes are for multiple servings.)

Sweet Simmered Shiitake

10 dried shiitake mushrooms • 3 Tbsp soy sauce • 2 Tbsp each sugar, sake, and mirin

1. Soak the shiitake in cold water until soft (1 hour). Remove the stems.
2. Put the shiitake in a pot with water to cover. Bring to a boil, then reduce heat and add all the other ingredients. Continue simmering until the liquid is almost completely absorbed.

Tora Mame

1 cup tora-mame (beans) • 1 cup sugar • 2 tsp soy sauce
Same procedure as for Adzuki Beans, this page.

Sweet Soybeans

1 cup soybeans • 1 cup sugar • 1 tsp soy sauce

1. Rinse the soybeans and cover with 3 cups water. Soak overnight.
2. Bring beans to a boil with their soaking water. Reduce heat. Skimming the top of the pot, simmer for an hour, adding water as needed.
3. When the beans are tender enough to crush in your fingers, add water to about the depth of the beans. Stir in the sugar and simmer over low heat for 20 minutes.
4. Add the soy sauce, cook briefly, and remove from heat.
★ The beans can be frozen in portions with their liquid for up to 2–3 weeks.

Adzuki Beans

1 cup adzuki beans • 1 cup sugar • 2 tsp soy sauce

1. Rinse the adzuki beans and cover with 3 cups water. Soak overnight.
2. Bring beans to a boil with their soaking water. Reduce heat, simmer for 4–5 minutes, and drain. Cover with fresh water and cook for 30–40 minutes.
3. When the beans are tender enough to crush in your fingers, add the sugar and simmer over low heat for 15 minutes.
4. Add the soy sauce, cook briefly, and remove from heat.

Black Beans

1 cup black beans • 1 cup sugar • 1 Tbsp soy sauce

1. Cook the beans as in step 1 and 2 of the Adzuki Beans recipe.
2. When the beans can be crushed, add or subtract water to about the depth of the beans. Stir in the sugar and simmer over low heat for 15 minutes.
3. Add the soy sauce, cook briefly, and remove from heat.

Quick Daikon-Carrot Pickles

½ daikon (about 16 oz; 500 g) • ¼ carrot • 1 tsp salt • 5 Tbsp vinegar • 1 Tbsp sugar

1. Cut the daikon and carrot into 1½" (4 cm) julienne.
2. Sprinkle with salt and let stand. Knead gently, then squeeze out the liquid.
3. Combine the vinegar and sugar and stir into the daikon mixture. Put a plate on top of the mixture to press lightly. Let stand for 30 minutes or more to develop the flavors.

Seaweed Topping

5 sheets roasted seaweed • 1 dried red pepper • 4 Tbsp soy sauce • 1 Tbsp sake • ½ Tbsp sugar • ½ Tbsp mirin

1. Tear the seaweed into small pieces. Place in a strainer and dip in cold water. Soak the red pepper in warm water and remove the seeds.
2. Drain the seaweed and place in a pot with all other ingredients. Boil, stirring occasionally, for 6–7 minutes.

Ginger Daikon

1 oz (30 g) dried daikon strips (kiriboshi-daikon) • 1" (3 cm) konbu • 1" (3 cm) carrot, julienned • 1 small piece ginger, julienned • ½ cup vinegar • 1 Tbsp dashi stock • 1½ Tbsp sugar • 2 tsp soy sauce • ½ tsp salt

1. Rinse and scrub the daikon strips. Soak in cold water. Soak the konbu in cold water also and julienne.
2. Combine the daikon, konbu, carrot, and ginger. Mix the remaining ingredients and stir into the daikon mixture. Let stand 30 minutes or more to develop the flavors.

Stewed Konbu

1 oz (30 g) konbu • 3 Tbsp soy sauce • 1 Tbsp sugar • 1 Tbsp mirin • 1 Tbsp sake • 2 tsp vinegar • ¾ cup water

1. Soak the konbu in cold water.
2. Bring to a boil with all remaining ingredients. Reduce heat to a simmer and cook for 15 minutes.
3. Remove the konbu and julienne, then return to the pot and simmer for 2–3 minutes more.

Chrysanthemum Turnips

7–8 small turnips, peeled • 1 Tbsp salt • 5 Tbsp vinegar • 1 Tbsp sugar • 1 dried red pepper

1. Trim off the top and bottom of the turnip. Make thin criss-cross diagonal incisions from the top almost all the way through to the bottom, so as to create the petals of a chrysanthemum.
2. Soak the turnips in 1 cup of warm salted water until soft. Rinse and gently squeeze out the water.
3. Combine the vinegar and sugar. Marinate the turnip and the red pepper in the vinegar mixture for at least an hour.

Stewed Liver

7 oz (200 g) chicken livers and heart • 3–4 slices ginger • ½ naganegi (Japanese bunching onion), chopped • 3 Tbsp soy sauce • 1 Tbsp mirin • 1 Tbsp sake • ½ Tbsp sugar

1. Remove the fat from the liver. Cut the heart in half and remove the blood clots. Combine and boil for 3–4 minutes. Rinse in cold water and drain.
2. Combine the liver mixture, the ginger, and the naganegi in a pot with water to cover. Add the remaining ingredients.
3. Bring to a boil. Reduce heat and cook until the liquid is absorbed.

Cod Roe Sprinkles

1 sac salted cod roe

1. Make a slit in the sac so that it will not explode.
2. Wrap loosely in plastic wrap and heat for 3 minutes in a microwave oven(*) until cooked through.
3. Remove the sac and place the eggs in strainer. Push the roe through the strainer with the back of a spoon.

(*)The cooking time is for a 500-watt microwave oven.

Sardine Sprinkles

2 oz (50 g) young sardines (chirimenjako)

1. Dry-roast the sardines over low heat in a heavy pan. Do not let them burn.
2. Chop.

Miso Peanuts

4 oz (100 g) gobo (burdock root) • Ginger to taste • 2 Tbsp cooking oil • 2 oz (50 g) peanuts • 5 Tbsp miso • 3 Tbsp sugar • 1 Tbsp mirin

1. Using a vegetable peeler, cut the gobo into short, thin strips. Rinse in cold water and drain. Julienne the ginger.
2. Sauté the gobo and ginger in the cooking oil. When tender, stir in the peanuts.
3. Stir in the miso, sugar, and mirin.

Shrimp Sprinkles

2/3 oz (20 g) dried shrimp (sakura-ebi)

1. Dry-roast the shrimp over low heat in a heavy pan. Do not let them burn.
2. Sift through a strainer. Chop the remaining pieces.

Tricolor Vegetables

4 oz (100 g) cauliflower florets • 1/2 carrot, peeled • 1 Japanese cucumber • 1 tsp salt • 1/2 cup vinegar • 1 Tbsp sugar • 2 Tbsp hot water

1. Blanch the cauliflower. Slice the carrot into 1/4" (5 mm) rounds. If available, use a vegetable cutter to create flower shapes. Boil until almost tender. Cut the cucumber into 1 1/2" (4 cm) lengths. Rub with 1/2 tsp of the salt.
2. Combine the remaining salt, the vinegar, the sugar, and the hot water. Marinate the vegetables in this mixture for at least an hour. Before serving, slice the cucumbers into smaller pieces.

Turnip-Leaf Sprinkles

4 oz (100 g) turnip greens • 1 Tbsp white sesame seeds • 1/2 tsp salt

1. Boil the turnip in salted water and plunge in cold water. Squeeze out the water and chop fine.
2. Place in a heavy pan and dry roast slowly, stirring with 4–5 chopsticks to separate.
3. Add the sesame seeds and salt and roast briefly.

QUICK SOUP THREE WAYS

These soup ingredients and hot water make any bento into a satisfying meal.

Plum-Konbu Soup

Cut *2–3 pieces of Stewed Konbu* (p. 61) into squares. Remove the seed from *1 umeboshi (pickled plum)* and chop. Combine in the container.

Miso Soup with Wakame

Miso Ball: Combine *1 Tbsp miso, chopped naganegi,* and *1/5 package (1 g) bonito flakes* and form into a ball. Place on a skewer or fork and roast on all sides over a flame. Put *chopped dried wakame* with the Miso Ball in the container.

Bacon Soup

Thinly slice *1/4 onion.* Julienne *1 slice of bacon* crosswise. Sauté in *1 tsp cooking oil.* Stir in *1 Tbsp miso* and *1 tsp sake.* Add *chopped steamed spinach.*

When ready to eat, place the soup mixture in a soup bowl or mug. Add hot water. Stir gently (the Miso Ball should dissolve in the hot water) and enjoy.